# THE SEVEN WONDERS
## OF THE MEDIEVAL WORLD

Reg Cox & Neil Morris

Belitha Press

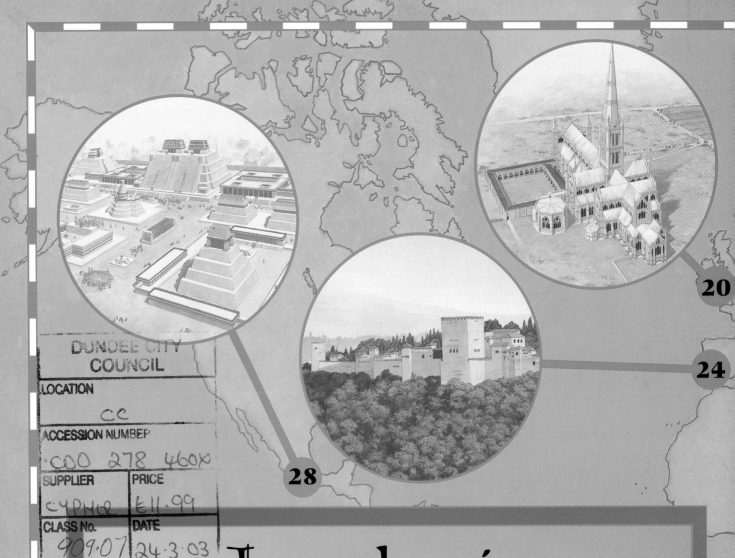

20

24

28

# Introduction

The famous Wonders of the Ancient World were first listed by an ancient Greek poet. His list has survived to this day, but no such list exists for other periods of history. The wonders chosen for this book belong to the thousand years of history starting in about AD 500. In Europe this period was called the Middle Ages. It began with the fall of the Western Roman Empire and brings us up to 1500, when modern times began. The word 'medieval' describes the Middle Ages and refers to Europe. But, as you will see, exciting things were happening all over the world.

# Contents

Words in bold are explained in the glossary on page 32.

**16**

**4**

**12**

**8**

# Cave of Ten Thousand Buddhas

**T**his is one of a series of cave temples carved into the hills along the banks of the Yishui River in eastern China. The temples are called the Longmen Caves, and are **dedicated** to the **Buddha**, the Indian prince whose teachings founded the religion of Buddhism.

## THE FIRST CAVES

Work began on the Longmen Caves in AD 494, when the Chinese emperor moved the capital of his empire to Luoyang, in the modern province of Henan. The caves are 12 kilometres south of Luoyang, which today is a busy city of over a million people.

## CHINESE BUDDHISM

Buddhism arrived in China hundreds of years before the caves were begun. In AD 67 the emperor of the Han **dynasty** sent messengers to India to collect Buddhist scriptures. On their way the messengers met two Indian Buddhist monks, who gave them both scriptures and statues. The four returned to Luoyang and built China's first Buddhist temple.

## CARVED IN ROCK
The Longmen temples and sculptures are carved from the dense grey limestone of the area. The caves contain about 100,000 Buddhist statues. Fengxian Temple is the biggest shrine. It has a seated Buddha over 17 metres high, which is about the same as a very tall tree.

## TANG DYNASTY ART
The Cave of Ten Thousand Buddhas, called Wanfo dong in Chinese, was hollowed out in 680. This was early in the Tang dynasty, which lasted from 618 to 907.

## TEN THOUSAND BUDDHAS
The cave is square, and on the side walls are the thousands of tiny statues that give the cave its name. These are carved in **bas-relief**. There is also a large Buddha surrounded by four followers. Alongside the tiny Buddhas are images of musicians playing flutes, cymbals, harps and other stringed instruments. The carvers were able to make the images very fine and detailed because the limestone was so dense.

The art of Buddhist cave sculpture died out in the ninth century, as the Tang dynasty came to an end.

*This life-sized statue (above) stands at the entrance to Wanfo dong Cave.*

5

One of the many pieces of silk found in the Longmen Caves shows monks kneeling before Buddha.

A guardian king of Buddhism carved on the wall of Fengxian Temple.

## Cave of Ten Thousand Buddhas ◆

Below are some of the famous ten thousand Buddhas. These small seated statues are near the entrance to Wanfo dong Cave.

The narrow, high-roofed Guyang Cave was probably the first of the Longmen Caves to be carved, soon after AD 494.

The Fengxian Temple took three years to build and was finished in AD 675. Next to the colossal Buddha there are **disciples** and divine beings. The roof of the cave has been worn away.

Followers guard the large Buddha in Wanfo dong (right). The ceiling is made up of a huge carved lotus flower, which has the date on it.

A standing Buddha in one of the three Binyang Caves, which are a few minutes' walk from the Wanfo dong Cave.

# Great Zimbabwe

T he modern country of Zimbabwe takes its name from the huge site of stone ruins, known as Great Zimbabwe. **Archaeologists** believe that the stone ruins were probably at the centre of a great African empire for hundreds of years.

## STONE HOUSES

In the African Bantu language, Zimbabwe means 'stone houses'. In fact the stone was used to make enclosures around buildings made of a mud mixture. The oldest parts of the ruins date from the eighth century, but people probably lived at the site for 600 years before then. From about 1100 the whole region was ruled by the Shona people, who today still make up a large part of the population of Zimbabwe and Mozambique.

## GOLD TRADERS

The original settlers were farmers, but Great Zimbabwe became more important when people who were cattle breeders arrived. They were probably also traders. The empire was at its height from the twelfth to the fifteenth century. We know from the remains that the people who lived there were skilled miners and craftsmen. They mined and **smelted** gold, which they traded with Arab, Indian and Chinese travellers.

## RICH SEA PORTS

They also traded ivory, iron and tortoise shells, in exchange for cotton, silk, glass beads, spices and porcelain. Great Zimbabwe was probably also a slave centre, used to transport Africans to Arab lands. Goods flowed through large ports on the shores of the Indian Ocean. Sixteenth-century European traders wrote of citizens dressed in fine silks and cottons.

## REMAINS OF THE SITE

About 150 ruling adults may have lived in Great Zimbabwe at its height, with thousands of people settled around it. A stone **enclosure**, 250 metres round, is the main structure left at the site. Inside are the foundations of many small mud buildings, as well as a round tower that stands 9 metres high. This may have been used in ceremonies. The enclosure is overlooked by a nearby hill fortress, with more small enclosures.

## MODERN REDISCOVERY

We do not know why the city fell into ruin, but drought and famine may have played a part. It was used until the seventeenth century, and then was rediscovered by Europeans in 1867. At first people thought they might find King Solomon's gold mines there, which were mentioned in the Bible. They dug up land, adding to the damage of time and destroying clues to the city's past.

*This figure of a bird, carved out of* **soapstone** *and sitting on a pillar, was found at the site.*

This pair of welded iron gongs was found at one of the many small ruined sites between the Great Enclosure and the hill fortress.

A mould carved from soapstone. It was used to cast cross-shaped copper **ingots**, like those below. The ingots may have been used as money.

The solid round tower stays in place without **mortar**, like all the stone structures at the site. The tower may have been built to look like a grain bin, a symbol of food and plenty. But its exact purpose remains a mystery.

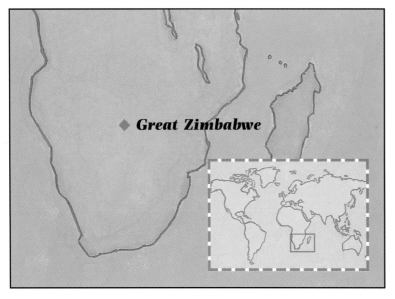

♦ **Great Zimbabwe**

Next to the copper ingots are two pointed iron arrowheads. Below them are iron mining tools, a knife and a spearhead.

Few of Great Zimbabwe's gold ornaments have been found. This golden rhinoceros was found at a site further south.

An iron spoon discovered outside the enclosure. It was probably brought by a trader from the East African coast.

The Zimbabwe people liked carving animals. The rim of this soapstone dish shows a baboon, a dog, a man, a bird and a zebra.

Curved steps in the outer wall form the northern entrance to the Great Enclosure. There were two other entrances, as well as an inner wall.

This female figure, carved from soapstone, stood in a stone or mud base. It may have been used in ceremonies where people worshipped their ancestors.

The outer wall of the Great Enclosure is almost 10 metres high in places. It is made of nearly a million granite blocks. In places it is decorated with rows of zigzags, a common African pattern.

# Angkor Wat

A ngkor Wat is the finest temple of the ruined city of Angkor in north-west Cambodia. Angkor was built as the capital of the once great **Khmer** empire, and the temple covers an area of nearly 2.5 square kilometres.

## CITY IN THE JUNGLE

In 1850 a French missionary, hacking his way through dense tropical forest in Cambodia, was amazed to come across the ruins of a magnificent city. More than a hundred temples had been crumbling away in the jungle for over four centuries. Archaeologists soon arrived to explore and restore this city of temples.

## KHMER KINGS

From the eighth to the thirteenth centuries, Khmer kings ruled a powerful civilization in South-East Asia. This began to grow even greater when Jayavarman II became king in AD 802. He ruled for 60 years and moved his capital many times. Finally he chose the area of Angkor and started to build on a large scale.

## ON THE EDGE OF A LAKE

Angkor, which means 'city' in the Khmer language, was built near the northern shores of Tonle Sap (Great Lake). This large shallow lake feeds a tributary of the Mekong River, and was full of fish and surrounded by fertile soil.

## USING THE LAKE

Water from the lake helped to make Angkor a wealthy city. Khmer farmers used **irrigation** canals to help them grow three crops of rice each year. This meant that there was more food for more people. By AD 1000, more than half a million people may have lived in the great city's streets and squares.

## SURYAVARMAN'S TEMPLE

The temple of Angkor Wat was built for King Suryavarman II early in the twelfth century, and was dedicated to the **Hindu** god Vishnu. The three-storey building contains a series of rectangular enclosures. Its towers, shaped like lotus buds, rise to a height of 60 metres.

## TOMB FOR A KING

The temple's corridors are lined with sculptures and carvings showing scenes from ancient myths. The building is surrounded by two sets of walls. A wide moat was fed by one of the city's two large reservoirs, which were used mainly to water the crops during the dry season.

When Suryavarman died, his temple was used as his tomb.

## THE END OF ANGKOR

In 1431 the city of Angkor was attacked and destroyed by Thai warriors. The ruined city was left to be overgrown by the jungle, until it was found again 150 years ago.

*A stone lion stands guard. There may originally have been as many as 300 of them at Angkor Wat.*

This head adorned the temple of Bayon. This was built in the thirteenth century for Jayavarman VII, the last great king of Angkor.

The main entrance to Angkor Wat, as it looks today. About 5,000 craftsmen and 50,000 other workers helped to build the temple.

Heavenly dancers appear on the walls of Angkor Wat. These graceful creatures were said to have been born on the spray of ocean waves.

Suryavarman II, who brought peace to the Khmer Kingdom. He died around 1150. People thought he was a god-king, sent from heaven.

Angkor Wat was a symbol for the five-peaked Mount Meru, home of the Hindu gods. The central tower is the tallest of the five towers.

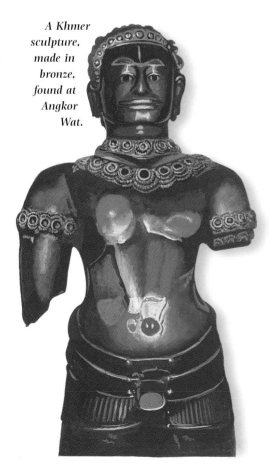

A Khmer sculpture, made in bronze, found at Angkor Wat.

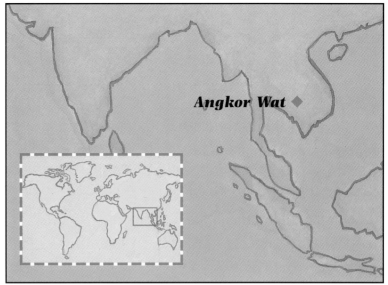

Angkor Wat ◆

Many of Angkor's sculptures, such as these divine figures, are in relief, which means that they are carved out of a flat background.

This life-like battle scene is full of action, as foot soldiers fight alongside warriors mounted on elephants. These reliefs record Khmer history.

# Krak des Chevaliers

T his castle in Syria is one of the best examples of medieval military **architecture** in the world. It was built by the Christian **crusaders**, who fought to recapture the Holy Land from the **Muslims**, followers of the religion of Islam.

## MUSLIM STRONGHOLD

Syria is on one of the world's oldest trade routes from the Far East to Europe, and throughout history people have fought over the region. Around AD 640, the Arabs conquered Syria and made it the centre of their empire. Most Syrians became Muslim, and for many years Muslims and Christians lived alongside one another.

But in the eleventh century the Turks, who had converted to the Muslim faith, took over much of the area. They became more and more hostile to Christian **pilgrims**. From 1095 onwards, crusaders travelled from Europe to fight the Muslims. In 1142 crusading knights captured a Muslim stronghold at Qal'at al-Hosen, which had been built to protect a route to and from the Mediterranean Sea. The conquering soldiers were Knights of the Hospital of St John of Jerusalem, sometimes called Knights Hospitallers.

## CASTLE OF THE KNIGHTS

Qal'at al-Hosen was in a very important place for the crusaders, and they set about building a large, powerful fortress on a hill 650 metres above sea level. The fortress was later called Krak des Chevaliers, which is French-Arabic for 'castle of the knights'.

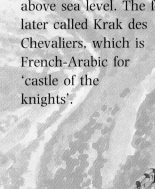

## TOWERED WALLS

Krak des Chevaliers was almost impossible to attack. It had two high walls and 13 towers. The inner wall was higher than the outer wall, and they were separated by a moat and a steep slope. The fortress covers 3,000 square metres and could hold a **garrison** of 2,000 soldiers with their horses, fighting equipment and enough food to last for five years.

## INSIDE THE WALLS

Inside the inner wall were **vaulted** halls, chapels, workshops, storerooms, and a maze of passages and walkways. It was like a small, armoured city. The crusaders held their castle for well over 100 years, through many conflicts. Then in 1271, after a month of fierce fighting, it finally fell to Baybars, the Muslim sultan of Syria and Egypt.

This view of Krak shows how well its solid walls have survived. It is one of the strongest castles ever built.

The **coat of arms** of the Knights Hospitallers, showing Saint Mary, Saint Peter, Saint Catherine and Saint Mary Magdalene.

Krak had its own **aqueduct**, a narrow bridge that acted as a canal. Water flowed across it to fill the castle's reservoirs and supply the soldiers with drinking water.

Plan of Krak des Chevaliers

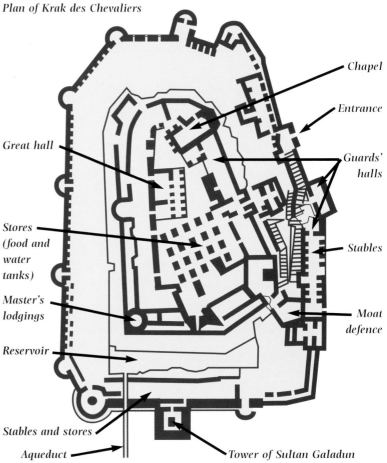

Chapel

Entrance

Guards' halls

Great hall

Stables

Stores (food and water tanks)

Master's lodgings

Moat defence

Reservoir

Stables and stores

Aqueduct

Tower of Sultan Galadun

Different parts of the castle were connected by vaulted tunnels and covered passageways. Knights could move quickly between towers and halls.

**Krak des Chevaliers** ◆

*A mounted **Saracen** fights a crusader. Krak's defenders were finally tricked into surrendering by a forged letter.*

The **loggia** was a covered gallery next to the great hall. This vaulted hall was the castle's main dining and meeting room.

*Knights Hospitallers began as a **religious order** who treated wounded soldiers. They later became a fighting force.*

# Salisbury Cathedral

The famous cathedral at Salisbury, in southern England, was built in the thirteenth century. Hundreds of medieval masons and carpenters worked with amazing skill to create this beautiful building.

## OLD SARUM

The story of the cathedral begins on a hill near Stonehenge – first the site of an Iron Age camp and then a Roman settlement. In 1075, the Normans built a castle and a small cathedral on the site, which they called Sarum. But there were disagreements between the people in the castle and the cathedral. Eventually the cathedral's bishop, Herbert Poore, decided to build a new cathedral in a valley to the south, where he owned water meadows. At Old Sarum there had been no good supply of water, so the new site was a better one.

## FIRM FOUNDATION

The bishop died before building work began. His brother, Richard Poore, became the next bishop, and was given the Pope's permission to carry out the plan. He decided to build the cathedral of Chilmark stone, which was brought by cart from a mine almost 20 kilometres away. The foundation stones were laid in 1220. The cathedral's foundations are little more than a metre deep. This is because they rest on a large natural foundation – a layer of flint gravel.

## COMPLETING THE CATHEDRAL

In 1225 the first three altars were **dedicated**, and the completed chapel was partitioned off from the building work, so that daily services could be held. The main building took another 33 years to complete, and the cathedral was **consecrated** in 1258.

A community called New Sarum grew around the cathedral, and today we know this as the city of Salisbury.

## TOWER AND SPIRE

Between 1285 and 1315 a tower and spire were added to the cathedral. An amazing 6,500 tonnes of stone were used to build these. The extra weight buckled the four pillars that supported the tower and spire, and **buttresses** and arches were put in to help take the weight. Almost four centuries later the spire was checked by Christopher Wren, who found that it was leaning 75 centimetres off centre. Iron rods were used to strengthen it, and since then it has not moved. The spire is 123 metres high, the tallest in Britain.

*The seal of Richard Poore (above), who was Bishop of Sarum from 1217 to 1228.*

A view down the length of the cathedral today, looking through the **nave** towards the great west window. The cathedral is 144 metres long, and the nave is 25 metres high.

This cross section shows how the spire was built around wooden scaffolding. The wood is still there today.

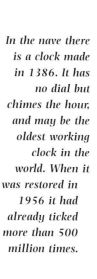

In the nave there is a clock made in 1386. It has no dial but chimes the hour, and may be the oldest working clock in the world. When it was restored in 1956 it had already ticked more than 500 million times.

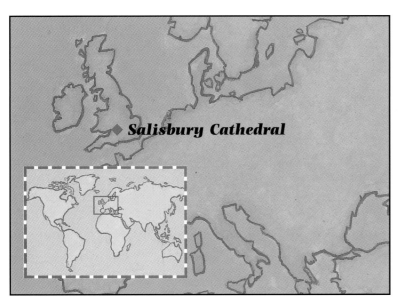

This stone dog lies at his master's feet on the tomb of Robert, Lord Hungerford, who died in 1459. The cathedral has many famous tombs.

Workers used a **windlass** to haul stone blocks up to the tower when the spire was being built. The original wooden windlass is still in the cathedral.

This thirteenth-century sculpture shows Adam and Eve in the Garden of Eden. The cathedral was once full of colourful wall paintings and sculptures, but many of them have faded.

The tomb of William Longespée, Earl of Salisbury, who laid one of the cathedral's foundation stones. He was the first person to be buried in the chapel, in 1226.

# Alhambra

This famous **citadel** stands above the city of Granada, in the Andalusian region of southern Spain. It was built on a high plateau and was the last **stronghold** of the Moorish kings of Granada. The citadel had strong walls around it, with 23 towers and four gates.

### AN ANCIENT STRONGHOLD

The Moors were Arab and Berber people from an ancient region called Mauretania, in North Africa. They were Muslims, and they invaded Spain in the eighth century. At Granada the Moorish warriors built a fortress on the remains of an ancient stronghold called Alcazaba. They strengthened the original fortress with high walls, towers and ramparts.

### THE RED FORT

The Moors called their new citadel Al-Qal'a al-Hambra, which means 'the red fort'. This Arabic name probably came from the colour of the sun-dried bricks that were used to build the outer walls. Its Spanish name was then later shortened to Alhambra.

### A BEAUTIFUL PALACE

The Alhambra was a military fortress, with offices, houses, shops, mosques, a **royal mint**, a garrison of soldiers, a prison, public baths and a hospital. But in the thirteenth and fourteenth centuries, especially during the reign of King Yusuf I, it was developed into a beautiful palace. There were columns and arches, and the rooms were full of patterns and decoration.

## COURTYARDS AND TERRACES

The Moorish architects built wonderful sunny courtyards surrounded by shady arcades and terraces. The gardens, with their fountains and plants, made the palace seem light, cool and scented. The beautiful Court of the Myrtles is overlooked by the Tower of Comares, which rises above the Hall of the Ambassadors. King Yusuf received foreign visitors in this grand reception room.

## FALL OF THE MOORS

The Moors ruled large parts of Spain for more than 700 years. But over the centuries Spanish Christians recaptured their territory. They finally drove the Muslims out of their last stronghold, Alhambra, in 1492.

## RUIN AND RESTORATION

Parts of the Alhambra were ruined in the final struggle between the Moors and the Christians. Some of the rooms were damaged over time, and in the sixteenth century King Charles V of Spain had parts of the palace rebuilt in a more Italian style. In 1812 some towers were destroyed by soldiers, and nine years later an earthquake caused further damage. In recent years much of this Moorish citadel, with its palace and gardens, has been restored.

*This carved ivory box has the delicate decoration and symmetrical patterns often used by the Moors. The box is 18 centimetres high.*

The beautiful domed ceiling in the Hall of the Two Sisters. The hall was named after two sisters who, imprisoned there, pined away and died.

There are poems, quotations from the **Koran** and other Islamic inscriptions everywhere. This one appears at the top of a column.

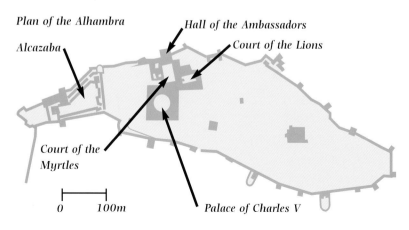

Plan of the Alhambra

Alcazaba

Hall of the Ambassadors

Court of the Lions

Court of the Myrtles

Palace of Charles V

0    100m

This sword and leather scabbard are decorated in the Moorish style. They belonged to Muhammad XI, the last Moorish king of Granada.

The Court of the Lions is named after 12 stone lions that support a fountain. Water pours from the lions' mouths.

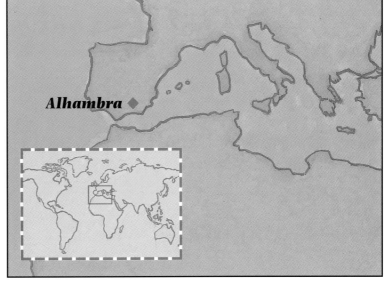

Alhambra ◆

In this splendid palace, decorated arches create a honeycomb effect of light, and windows look out on beautiful walled gardens.

Walls were painted, gilded and decorated with geometric patterns of coloured tiles.

The peaceful Court of the Myrtles contains a fishpond lined by myrtle hedges.

# Tenochtitlan

Tenochtitlan began as a settlement of reed huts. It became a great city and the centre of the powerful Aztec empire for almost 200 years. It stood in the south of present-day Mexico, and its ruins lie beneath modern Mexico City.

## THE EAGLE, THE CACTUS AND THE SNAKE

The early Aztec people were Indian hunters who wandered the deserts of northern Mexico. They moved south to the fertile Valley of Mexico in about 1200. According to legend, their sun god, Huitzilopochtli, told them to settle where they found a special sign – an eagle on a cactus grasping a snake. In about 1325 the Aztecs found what they were looking for, on a marshy island in Lake Texcoco. They built a village there, and called it Tenochtitlan, 'the place of the prickly-pear cactus'.

## CITY OF CANALS

The Aztecs reclaimed and created land. They extended their island by dredging mud from the bottom of the shallow lake and building reed platforms. These floating gardens were very fertile and were used to grow vegetables. Drinking water was brought in by aqueduct. By about 1415 Tenochtitlan had grown into a city, with stone houses, temples and palaces. Like Venice today, it was a city of islands connected by canals and linked to the mainland by raised paths.

## PYRAMID TEMPLES

Between 100,000 and 500,000 people may have lived in Tenochtitlan. By 1500 it was probably the largest city in the world. In the central square, surrounded by a wall, was a 30-metre-high pyramid with staircases leading up to two temples. These were decorated with carvings and paintings. One temple belonged to Huitzilopochtli, and the other to Tlaloc, the rain god. Here priests used stone knives to sacrifice people to the gods by cutting out their hearts.

## END OF AN EMPIRE

The Spaniards who sailed to America in the sixteenth century were amazed by the wealth and splendour of the Aztecs. They noticed too how clean the Aztecs kept the city. Roads were swept and rubbish was taken away in barges.

The Spanish conquerors soon attacked. The Aztec emperor, Montezuma, was killed, and in 1521 Tenochtitlan was destroyed. This was the end of the Aztec empire. Mexico City, the largest city in the world today, was built on the ruins of the once great city of Tenochtitlan.

*The Aztec sun god Huitzilopochtli (left) was also the god of war and **patron** of the city of Tenochtitlan.*

29

The Aztec emperor wore a feathered head-dress when he appeared in public, as well as fine jewellery.

This carving (left) shows a symbol of Tlaloc, god of rain. His teeth point down towards the growing plants.

A golden mask (right) of Xipe Totec, god of spring, and patron of metalworkers.

The fertile gardens of Xochimilco, south of Mexico City, are all that is left of the original Aztec floating gardens.

This picture from a sacred Aztec book, or codex, shows the legend of how the city was founded. Tribal chieftains surround the eagle and cactus.

This fourteenth-century Aztec stone carving shows an eagle perched on a cactus with a snake in its claws.

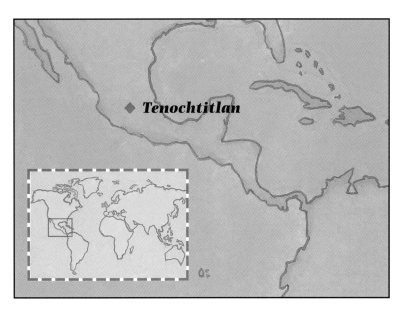

A knife used to sacrifice people. Captured enemy warriors were killed to please the gods and feed them with blood from the human heart.

This carved Aztec stone, over 3 metres wide, was found beneath Mexico City in 1790. The face in the centre may be the sun. The symbols show the beginning and end of the Aztec world. The Aztecs believed the world had been created four times and that they were living in the fifth and last creation.

# GLOSSARY

**aqueduct:** a narrow bridge that carries water.

**archaeologist:** a person who studies the ancient past by digging up and looking at remains.

**architecture:** designing and putting up buildings.

**bas-relief:** figures and images that stand out slightly from the background rock.

**Buddha:** the Indian prince whose teachings founded the religion of Buddhism.

**buttress:** a stone wall support.

**citadel:** a fortified group of buildings.

**coat of arms:** the symbol of a family or group.

**consecrate:** to declare holy.

**crusaders:** Christian knights who fought to recapture the Holy Land from Muslims.

**dedicate:** to devote to holy use.

**disciple:** a follower of a teacher or a set of beliefs.

**dynasty:** a series of rulers, often coming from the same family.

**enclosure:** a wall surrounding a piece of land.

**garrison:** troops who guard a fortress.

**Hindu:** relating to Hinduism, the main religion of India.

**ingot:** a piece of metal cast from a mould.

**irrigation:** watering land to help crops grow.

**Khmer:** a people and civilization of Cambodia that were powerful from the eighth to the thirteenth centuries.

**Koran:** the sacred book of Islam.

**loggia:** a covered gallery.

**mason:** a person skilled in building with stone.

**mortar:** a cement-like mixture.

**Muslim:** a follower of the religion of Islam.

**nave:** the main section of a church.

**order:** a group of people with a special purpose.

**patron:** the guardian of a city, country or people.

**pilgrim:** a person who travels to a holy place.

**royal mint:** a place where money is made.

**Saracen:** a Muslim who fought against crusaders.

**smelt:** to get metal from ore by heating.

**soapstone:** a soft, greasy type of stone.

**stronghold:** a fortress.

**vaulted:** with an arched roof.

**windlass:** a wheel used for raising heavy weights.

# INDEX

This edition published in 2002 by
Belitha Press
A member of **Chrysalis** Books plc
64 Brewery Road, London N7 9NT

Copyright © in this format Belitha Press
Series devised by Reg Cox
Design copyright © Reg Cox
Text copyright © Neil Morris
Illustrations copyright © James Field

ISBN 1 84138 494 1

CIP Data for this book is available from the British Library

Printed in Hong Kong

Editor: Claire Edwards
Designed by: Cat & Mouse Design
Picture researcher: Juliet Duff
Consultant: Dr. Anne Millard

Picture acknowledgements: Ancient Art and Architecture: 6 top left, 22 top, 26 top, 27 bottom right. By permission of the British Library: cover (MS ADD 28681F9). Werner Forman Archive: 7 bottom right, 10 top left and 11 bottom left Robert Aberman, 30 bottom left, 31 top left. Robert Harding Picture Library: 14 top right, 15 top left, 18 top, 19 top right, 23 bottom.